A Private Limited Dream: Rule No 1

MUHAMMAD SHAHJAD S

DEDICATION

To my creator:

CONTENTS

ACKNOWLEDGMENTS

To my creator

INTRODUCTION

In this book, we will explore the idea of building a business on dreams. We will look at how entrepreneurs and business leaders have used their dreams and passions to create successful companies and organizations. We will also explore the challenges and struggles that come with building a business, and how to overcome them.

The Power of Dreams: Dreams have the power to inspire and motivate us to achieve great things. When we have a clear vision of what we want to achieve, we are more likely to put in the hard work and dedication required to make it a reality. In this book, we will look at some of the most successful entrepreneurs and business leaders who have used their dreams to build their companies. We will also explore how to develop a clear and compelling vision for your own business.

Overcoming Challenges: Starting and building a business is not easy. There will be challenges and obstacles along the way that you will need to overcome. In this book, we will explore some of the most common challenges that entrepreneurs and business leaders face. We will also look at strategies for overcoming these challenges, such as staying focused and persistent, building a strong support network, and developing a plan for success.

Building a Strong Team: No business can be successful without a strong team. In this book, we will explore the importance of building a team of individuals who share your vision and are dedicated to making your business a success. We will look at how to attract and retain top talent, and how to create a culture of collaboration and teamwork within your organization.

Staying True to Your Dreams: As your business

grows and evolves, it can be easy to lose sight of the dreams that inspired you to start it in the first place. In this book, we will explore how to stay true to your dreams and passions as you navigate the challenges of growing your business. We will also look at how to maintain the entrepreneurial spirit that inspired you to start your business, even as it becomes more established and successful.

1 THE POWER OF DREAMS

Dreams have the power to inspire and motivate us to achieve great things. When we have a clear vision of what we want to achieve, we are more likely to put in the hard work and dedication required to make it a reality. Having a dream or a vision is crucial for any entrepreneur or business leader, as it gives them a sense of purpose and direction. It is the foundation upon which a business is built, and it is what gives a business its unique identity.

Let's look at some of the most successful entrepreneurs and business leaders who have used their dreams to build their companies. For example, Steve Jobs had a dream to create a computer that was simple and elegant, and that dream led to the creation of the Macintosh computer. Similarly, Mark Zuckerberg had a dream to connect the world through a social network, and that dream led to the creation of Facebook. These examples demonstrate the power of having a dream or a vision and how it can lead to the creation of something truly extraordinary.

In addition to looking at real-life examples, try to develop a clear and compelling vision for your own business. It will help you understand that having a clear vision is a vital step in creating a successful business.

In my next book, I'll explain how to create a vision that is unique to your company and compelling enough to entice others to join you on your journey.

Furthermore, let's discuss the importance of aligning your vision with your values and passions. It is essential that the business aligns with the entrepreneur's values and passions, as it will make it much easier for people to stay committed and motivated over the long term.

Also, try to be bold and daring with your vision and not be afraid to think big and do challenging activities.

In conclusion, having a dream or a vision is crucial for any entrepreneur or business leader.

2 Overcoming Challenges

Starting and building a business is not easy, and there will be challenges and obstacles along the way that need to be overcome. These challenges can come in many forms, such as financial difficulties, lack of customers, competition, and even personal struggles. In this chapter, we will explore some of the most common challenges that entrepreneurs and business leaders face, and how to overcome them.

One of the biggest challenges that entrepreneurs face is financial difficulties. Starting a business requires a significant investment of time, money, and resources. Many entrepreneurs struggle to secure funding and may face financial difficulties in the early stages of their business. To overcome this challenge, entrepreneurs must develop a detailed business plan that includes a budget and a financial forecast. They should also explore different funding options such as venture capital, crowdfunding, and small business loans. Additionally, they should also learn how to manage their finances effectively, and be prepared to make sacrifices in order to keep their business afloat.

Another common challenge that entrepreneurs face is a lack of customers. Without customers, a business cannot survive. Entrepreneurs must work hard to attract and retain customers by understanding their needs and offering them a product or service that meets those needs. To overcome this challenge, entrepreneurs should focus on building a strong brand and creating a compelling marketing strategy. They should also build relationships with their customers and gather feedback to improve their products or services.

Competition is also a major challenge for entrepreneurs. The marketplace is constantly changing, and businesses must adapt to stay competitive. To overcome this challenge, entrepreneurs must stay on top of industry trends and be willing to innovate. They should also differentiate their products or services from those of their competitors and find a unique niche in the market.

Personal struggles are also a common challenge that entrepreneurs face. Starting and building a business can be an emotional and stressful journey, and entrepreneurs must be prepared to face these struggles. To overcome this challenge, entrepreneurs should develop a strong support network of family, friends, and mentors. They should also take care of their physical and mental health and find ways to manage stress.

Starting and building a business is not easy, and there will be challenges and obstacles along the way that need to be overcome.

3 Building a Strong Team

No business can be successful without a strong team. A team of dedicated and skilled individuals who share the same vision and values can make all the difference in the success of a business. In this chapter, we will explore the importance of building a team, and how to attract and retain top talent. Additionally, we will also look at how to create a culture of collaboration and teamwork within your organization.

The first step in building a strong team is to identify the skills and expertise that are needed for your business to succeed. This may include areas such as marketing, finance, operations, and technology. Once you have identified the skills and expertise that are needed, you can begin to recruit and hire the individuals who possess these skills. It is essential to hire individuals who share the same vision and values as your business, and who are dedicated to making your business a success.

Once you have assembled a strong team, the next step is to create an environment that fosters collaboration and teamwork. This includes creating opportunities for team members to work together, providing regular team-building activities, and encouraging open communication. A positive and supportive work environment can help to improve morale, increase productivity, and reduce employee turnover.

Another important aspect of building a strong team is to provide opportunities for professional development and growth. This can include providing training and education, as well as offering opportunities for advancement within the company. By investing in the development of your team members, you can ensure that they have the skills and knowledge they need to be successful and make valuable contributions to your business.

Finally, it is essential to retain top talent by providing competitive compensation and benefits packages, and by recognizing and rewarding the contributions of your team members. Employee retention is a key factor in the success of a business, and it is important to create an environment that is attractive to top talent and that encourages them to stay with the company.

It is important to assemble a team of individuals who share the same vision and values as your business, and who are dedicated to making your business a success.

4 Staying True to Your Dreams

As your business grows and evolves, it can be easy to lose sight of the dreams that inspired you to start it in the first place. The day-to-day demands of running a business can be overwhelming, and it can be difficult to maintain the entrepreneurial spirit that inspired you to start your business. In this chapter, we will explore how to stay true to your dreams and passions as you navigate the challenges of growing your business. We will also look at how to maintain the entrepreneurial spirit that inspired you to start your business, even as it becomes more established and successful.

One of the most important things to remember is the reason why you started your business. It is essential to keep your original vision and mission statement in mind, and to remind yourself of the passion and drive that inspired you to start your business. This will help you to stay focused and motivated, even when faced with challenges and obstacles.

Another important aspect of staying true to your dreams is to stay connected to your customers. The customers are the reason why your business exists, and it is important to remember that your business is about serving them. By staying connected to your customers, you can gain valuable insights into their needs and preferences, and you can use this information to improve your products and services. Additionally, by staying connected to your customers, you can maintain the entrepreneurial spirit that inspired you to start your business, by constantly looking for ways to innovate and improve your business.

It is also important to stay true to your values and beliefs. As your business grows, you will be faced with many decisions, and it can be tempting to compromise your values and beliefs in order to make a quick profit. However, it is important to remember that your values and beliefs are what make your business unique, and it is essential to stay true to them in order to maintain the integrity of your business.

Finally, it is important to surround yourself with the

right people. As your business grows, it is important to surround yourself with individuals who share your vision and values. This includes employees, advisors, and mentors. By surrounding yourself with individuals who share your vision and values, you can ensure that your business stays true to its original mission and vision.

By remembering the reason why you started your business, staying connected to your customers, staying true to your values and beliefs, and surrounding yourself with the right people, you can ensure that your business stays true to its original mission and vision

5 TAKE ACTION AND MAKE IT HAPPEN

Building a business on dreams is not easy, but it is incredibly rewarding. When you have a clear vision and a passion for what you are doing, you will be able to overcome any challenge and achieve great success. In this book, we have looked at the power of dreams, how to overcome challenges, and how to build a strong team. We have also explored how to stay true to your dreams and maintain the entrepreneurial spirit that inspired you to start your business in the first place.

We have seen how having a clear vision and a passion for what you are doing is the foundation of any successful business. Dreams have the power to inspire and motivate us to achieve great things, and entrepreneurs who have a clear vision are more likely to put in the hard work and dedication required to make it a reality. We have also learned that while starting a business is not easy, it is important to stay focused and persistent, build a strong support network, and develop a plan for success to overcome the challenges that come with building a business.

We have also learned the importance of building a strong team. A team of dedicated and skilled individuals who share the same vision and values can make all the difference in the success of a business. By creating an environment that fosters collaboration and teamwork, providing opportunities for professional development and growth, and investing in the retention of top talent, we can ensure that our business is well-positioned for success.

As businesses grow and evolve, it can be easy to lose sight of the dreams that inspired you to start it in the first place. However, we have learned that it is essential to stay true to our dreams and passions, by remembering the reason why we started our business, staying connected to our customers, staying true to our values and beliefs, and surrounding ourselves with the right people. By doing so, we can maintain the entrepreneurial spirit that inspired us to start our business, and achieve great success.

In conclusion, building a business on your dreams is a journey, and it's important to stay focused, and persistent, and never give up. It requires hard work, dedication, and a willingness to overcome challenges and obstacles. However, by having a clear vision and a passion for what you are doing, building a strong team, and staying true to your dreams, you can achieve great success and turn your dreams into reality. This book has provided a comprehensive guide on how to start and build a successful business based on your dreams, it's now up to you to take action and make it happen.

6 RULE NO 1.

Starting a business or making an investment can be risky, but there are steps that can be taken to mitigate those risks. One such method is to implement a 10-point system for business associations or investments. We will need to follow the rules.

GOALS

1. **Diversification:** Spread investments across a variety of industries and geographic locations to mitigate risk.
2. **Due Diligence:** Thoroughly research potential investments and business partners to identify potential risks and opportunities.
3. **Contractual Protections:** Use contracts to clearly define the rights and responsibilities of all parties involved and to protect against potential breaches.
4. **Insurance:** Purchase appropriate insurance policies to protect against potential liabilities.
5. **Risk Management:** Develop and implement a risk management plan to identify, assess, and mitigate potential risks.
6. **Compliance:** Ensure compliance with all relevant laws and regulations to avoid penalties and legal liabilities.
7. **Contingency Planning:** Develop plans to mitigate risks, such as business interruption insurance.
8. **Regular Monitoring:** Regularly monitor investments and business partners to identify potential risks and opportunities.
9. **Avoid over-leveraging:** Avoid taking on too much debt or over-leveraging investments to reduce the risk of financial distress.

10. **Continuously Evaluate:** Continuously evaluate and re-evaluate the risk and potential return of investments and partnerships, and make adjustments as necessary.

CONDITIONS

1. 30 % MATCH WITH AN EXISTING BUSINESS.

a. Established customer base: Starting a business that is 30% similar to an existing one allows you to tap into an established customer base and market.

b. Proven business model: By starting a business that is similar to an existing one, you can benefit from a proven business model and avoid some of the trial and error associated with starting a new business.

c. Reduced costs: By starting a business that is similar to an existing one, you may be able to reduce costs associated with market research and product development.

d. Brand recognition: If your business is similar to an existing one, you may be able to leverage the existing business's brand recognition and reputation to attract customers.

e. Established relationships: An existing business may have established relationships with suppliers, distributors, and other partners that you can take advantage of when starting your own business.

f. Industry expertise: Starting a business that is similar to an existing one allows you to benefit from the expertise and knowledge of the existing business and its owners, which can help you make smarter business decisions.

g. Access to resources: An existing business may have access to resources such as funding, equipment, and employees that you can take advantage of when starting your own business.

2. 50 % SUBJECT KNOWLEDGE FOR ONE BOARD MEMBER.

a. Expertise: Having a board member with 50% subject knowledge in the industry or field in which your business operates can provide valuable expertise and knowledge to help guide and inform business decisions.

b. Network: A board member with subject knowledge may have a network of contacts in the industry that can be beneficial for the business in terms of partnerships, collaborations, and potential business opportunities.

c. Industry insight: A board member with subject knowledge can provide valuable industry insight and analysis to help the business stay ahead of trends and anticipate potential challenges.

d. Strategic planning: A board member with subject knowledge can provide valuable input in strategic planning and help the business identify new opportunities and potential areas for growth.

e. Decision-making: A board member with subject knowledge can provide valuable input in decision-making and help the business make informed decisions that align with industry trends and best practices.

f. Risk management: A board member with subject knowledge can help the business identify and mitigate risks specific to the industry, and may be able to identify potential opportunities that others may not see.

g. Innovation: A board member with subject knowledge can help the business stay innovative and competitive by identifying new and emerging technologies, trends, and best practices that could benefit the business.

3. 20 % INVESTMENT FROM RM TO START THE BUSINESS.

a. Reduced financial risk: Starting a business or making an investment with only 20% of your own money can significantly reduce your financial risk, as you are not investing all of your own money.

b. Leverage: Investing only 20% of your own money allows you to leverage the remaining 80% from other investors, which can increase your potential returns.

c. Diversification: Investing only 20% of your own money allows you to spread your investment across multiple ventures, which can help diversify your portfolio and mitigate risk.

d. Shared responsibility: Investing only 20% of your own money means that you will be sharing the responsibilities and risks of the business or investment with other investors.

e. Access to additional resources: Investing only 20% of your own money allows you to access additional resources, such as capital, expertise, and connections, from other investors that can help your business or investment success.

f. Reduced pressure: Investing only 20% of your own money means that you will have less pressure on the business or investment to perform, as you will have less invested in it.

g. Reduced stress: Investing only 20% of your own money means that you will have less stress, as you will not be risking all of your own money.

4. ROI IN ONE YEAR.

a. Quick return on investment: Starting a business or making an investment with an expected return on investment (ROI) within one year can provide a quicker financial return than a long-term investment.

b. Short-term cash flow: A business or investment with a one-year ROI can provide short-term cash flow, which can be useful for funding other investments or business ventures.

c. Flexibility: A business or investment with a one-year ROI allows for more flexibility in terms of reinvesting the capital or using it for other purposes.

d. Reduced risk: A business or investment with a one-year ROI can be seen as a lower risk compared to a long-term investment, as it may be less likely to be affected by long-term market fluctuations or other risks.

e. Testing the waters: A one-year ROI can be a good way to test the waters with a new business or investment idea, without committing to a long-term investment.

f. Easier to measure: A one-year ROI can be easier to measure and track compared to a longer-term investment, making it easier to determine if the investment is performing as expected.

g. Opportunity cost: A one-year ROI can provide an opportunity to invest in other opportunities that may have a better ROI if the current investment doesn't perform well.

5. TOTAL LOSS DOESN'T AFFECT MORE THAN 10% OF RM'S CURRENT ASSETS.

a. Limited financial impact: Starting a business or making an investment where a total loss would not affect more than 10% of your current assets can provide peace of mind, knowing that the potential loss is limited and won't significantly impact your overall financial situation.

b. Reduced risk: Investing in a business or venture where the potential loss is limited to 10% of current assets can be seen as a lower risk compared to an investment where the potential loss could be much greater.

c. Flexibility: Having a limit on the potential loss of investment allows for more flexibility in terms of taking on additional investments or business ventures.

d. Confidence: Knowing that a total loss would not affect more than 10% of current assets can give confidence in making the investment and in managing the business.

e. Preservation of capital: A total loss that does not affect more than 10% of current assets allows for the preservation of a large portion of the initial capital invested.

f. Option to walk away: A total loss that does not affect more than 10% of current assets allows for the option to walk away from a losing investment or business without significant financial impact.

g. Ability to recover: A total loss that does not affect more than 10% of current assets allows for the ability to recover financially and to make new investments or business ventures.

6. MINIMUM BUSINESS SCALE OF UP TO 7 YEARS.

a. Long-term stability: Starting a business or making an investment with a minimum business scale of up to 7 years can provide long-term stability, as the business or investment will have time to establish itself and grow over time.

b. Sustainable growth: A minimum business scale of 7 years allows for sustainable growth, as the business or investment will have time to establish a solid foundation and build a steady customer base.

c. Time to recoup investment: A minimum business scale of 7 years allows for more time to recoup the initial investment, and potentially even see significant returns.

d. Potential for scalability: A minimum business scale of 7 years allows for the potential to scale the business or investment over time and increase profitability.

e. Long-term planning: A minimum business scale of 7 years allows for long-term planning and the ability to anticipate and adapt to changes in the market and industry.

f. Stronger reputation: A business that can sustain for 7 years will have a stronger reputation, which will help in attracting new customers and retaining existing ones.

g. Greater potential for return on investment: A minimum business scale of 7 years allows for a greater potential for return on investment as the business or investment has a longer period of time to generate revenue and grow.

7. 2-YEAR BUSINESS RELATIONSHIP WITH THE PROPOSED PARTNER.

a. Established trust: Starting a business or making an investment with a partner that you have a 2-year business relationship with can provide a level of trust and understanding that may not be present in a new business relationship.

b. Familiarity with business practices: Having a 2-year business relationship with a partner allows for a deeper understanding of their business practices, which can help to avoid potential misunderstandings and conflicts.

c. Established communication: A 2-year business relationship allows for established communication channels, which can make it easier to work together and make important business decisions.

d. Shared history: A 2-year business relationship provides a shared history, which can be beneficial when making decisions and assessing potential risks.

e. Proven track record: A 2-year business relationship with a partner allows for an assessment of their performance over time, which can provide insight into their capabilities and reliability.

f. Stronger collaboration: A 2-year business relationship allows for stronger collaboration, as the partners have had time to build trust, shared understanding, and a shared vision for the business.

g. Reduced Risk: A 2-year business relationship allows for a better understanding of the partner's financial stability and ability to meet financial obligations, which can reduce the risk of potential financial loss.

8. NO LOAN IS REQUIRED TO START A BUSINESS.

a. Reduced debt: Starting a business or making an investment without the need for a loan can reduce the amount of debt the business or investment carries, which can make it more financially stable in the long term.

b. Increased flexibility: Without the need for a loan, the business or investment has more flexibility in terms of using funds and making important business decisions.

c. Reduced interest costs: Not needing a loan to start a business or make an investment means that the business or investment will not be incurring interest costs, which can increase profitability.

d. Increased control: Starting a business or making an investment without the need for a loan can provide greater control over the business or investment, as the business or investment is not beholden to the terms and conditions of a loan.

e. More equity: Starting a business or making an investment with no loan can give more equity, which can be beneficial for the business or investment in terms of future financing.

f. Creditworthiness: Starting a business or making an investment without the need for a loan can demonstrate the creditworthiness of the business or investment, which can make it more attractive to potential investors or partners.

g. Avoiding covenants: Starting a business or making an investment without the need for a loan means avoiding loan covenants that can limit the flexibility of the business or investment in terms of operations or investments.

9. ONE KEY PERSON TO TAKE COMPLETE RESPONSIBILITY FOR THE BUSINESS.

a. Clear leadership: Having one key person take complete responsibility for the business can provide clear leadership and direction, making it easier to make important business decisions and stay focused on achieving the business's goals.

b. Accountability: Having one key person take complete responsibility for the business can ensure accountability and make it easier to identify and address any issues that arise.

c. Efficiency: Having one key person take complete responsibility for the business can increase efficiency, as all business decisions and responsibilities are centralized, rather than spread across multiple people.

d. Stronger decision-making: Having one key person take complete responsibility for the business can lead to stronger decision-making, as the person in charge has a deep understanding of the business and its goals.

e. Better communication: Having one key person take complete responsibility for the business can make it easier to communicate the business's vision and goals to employees and stakeholders.

f. Faster execution: Having one key person take complete responsibility for the business can lead to faster execution of business decisions, as there's no need to get consensus from multiple parties.

g. Easier to track progress: Having one key person take complete responsibility for the business makes it easier to track progress and measure the success of the business.

10. 90% VOTE APPROVAL FROM THE BOARD DIRECTORS.

a. Stronger consensus: Starting a business or making an investment with 90% vote approval from the board of directors can indicate strong consensus and support for the decision, which can increase the likelihood of success.

b. Reduced risk: A 90% vote approval from the board of directors can reduce the risk of a decision being challenged or reversed in the future.

c. Better decision-making: A 90% vote approval from the board of directors indicates that the decision has been thoroughly evaluated and discussed, which can lead to better decision-making.

d. Increased commitment: A 90% vote approval from the board of directors can indicate increased commitment from the board to the success of the business or investment.

e. Greater buy-in: A 90% vote approval from the board of directors can lead to greater buy-in from the board members, which can increase the chances of success.

f. Stronger accountability: A 90% vote approval from the board of directors can lead to stronger accountability, as the board is more likely to be committed to the success of the business or investment.

g. Better alignment: A 90% vote approval from the board of directors can lead to better alignment among the board members, which can result in better decision-making and a more cohesive approach to achieving the goals of the business.

RULE 1: Any business associations or investments must score 7/10 points under the conditions, and conditions 2 and 10 are mandator

ABOUT THE AUTHOR

Muhammad Shahjad is an Indian Entrepreneur